An Earth Child's Book of Verse

Written by Marian Louise Camden
Illustrated by Diane Beem Wright

This one is for Diane and Renee
with love and appreciation.

Sleep and Dream

When all the Earth's asleep,
When snow falls cold and deep,

When vale and hill are white,
When Stars keep watch at night:

Then peace has come to Earth,
Sweet sleep before new birth,

Soft dreams of days to come,
Fair songs soon to be sung;

When children laugh and run,
When Elders' tales are spun,

When Brother Sun is blessing,
With honey-warmth caressing,

Then Summer is our Queen,
Mother of all that is green.

Quickening

What is quickening, Mother?
What does quicken mean?
Quicken means the seed below
will soon be coming green.

Quicken is a magic word from many long years past;
Quicken means the winter cold will not forever last.
Branches quicken as little buds grow,
Spring flowers quicken in wet spring snow.

What is quickening, Father?
What does quickening do?
Quicken means the Sun will shine
in skies of brilliant blue.

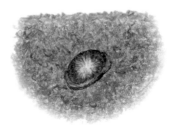

Quicken is a magic word from many long years past;
Quicken means the winter cold will not forever last.
Branches quicken as little buds grow,
Spring flowers quicken in wet spring snow.

When is Quickening, Grandma?
How will I then know?
When the cowslips raise their heads
above the melting snow.

Quicken is a magic word from many long years past;
Quicken means the winter cold will not forever last.
Branches quicken as little buds grow,
Spring flowers quicken in wet spring snow.

Wind and Water

March winds blow,
Cold waters flow,
I hear the river singing.

March winds blow
Quick scuds of snow,
I hear the river singing.

March winds blow,
The green trees show,
I hear the river singing.

March winds blow,
Mild jonquils grow,
Beside the river singing.

Lady Spring in the Meadow

Seed-stars dance, young rams prance,
all in the green meadow.
Flowers soak up springtime rain,
all in the green meadow.
Wheat we sow, green peas we grow,
all in the green meadow.

Spring is here, our Lady dear,
Come to bless us ever.
Spring is come, winter's done,
As scarlet grows the heather.

Children greet, lovers meet,
all in the green meadow.
Across the grass, sunbeams pass,
all in the green meadow.
Feast and dance, sweet romance,
all in the green meadow.

Spring is here, our Lady dear,
Come to bless us ever.
Spring is come, Winter's done,
As scarlet grows the heather.

Hawthorn Maypole Dance

'Round the hawthorn tree hang we
Ribbons pink and yellow,
Purple, green and blue and white,
Every lass and fellow.

Pink for love, bright gold for friends,
Purple's wisdom never ends;
Green to keep us safe at night,
Blue for goodness, white for light.

Take a hawthorn branch in bloom,
Hang it in the dairy room;
Strong and hale the cows shall grow,
Milk and cream shall overflow.

'Round the hawthorn tree hang we
Ribbons pink and yellow,
Purple, green and blue and white,
Every lass and fellow.

Place a hawthorn branch up high
In your cottage rafter,
Chase the bogey man away,
Gone forever after.

Tie some hawthorn on a post,
Where the travelers see it most
Luck you'll grant them on their way
Wish turned true be yours this day.

Underneath the hawthorn tree
Dark at midnight you may see,
Faeries feast and faeries dance,
Hush! They'll vanish at a glance.

'Round the hawthorn tree hang we
Ribbons pink and yellow,
Purple, green and blue and white,
Every lass and fellow.

Fire and Thunder Magic

Bonfire burns of holly logs
with leaping crimson flames;
Bumbling thunder grumbles, yet
brings blessing for the grains.

In hot July, the flowers flourish,
Water flows, our crops to nourish;
Sing of magic, herbs, and lore;
Burn ye bright stars evermore.

Flames go dancing, watch them whirl,
ye old and young together
Sing of summer's scorching heat for
fine corn-growing weather.

Herbs grow by the riverside;
Earth Folk gather them inside.
Sing of magic, herbs, and lore;
Burn ye bright fire evermore.

Bonfire laughs and leaps aloft,
red ruby flash his flames.
Bumbling thunder grumbles, yet
brings blessing for the grains.

What's a Peridot?

What's a peridot, Cousin? I don't know.
What's a peridot, Brother? I don't know!

Ancient stone of palest green,
What does your soft color mean?

Draw close child, so you may know,
Deep magic of the peridot.

Listen well so you will hear:
Safety, wisdom, healing, cheer,
Lovers, strength, and prophecy,
Finally, most importantly,
Peridot is friendship's friend,
Putting envy to an end.

Come to the Harvest-- Hurry!

Ripe corn grows heavy in the field.
Come to the harvest--hurry!
Fruit and nut offer their yield.
Come to the harvest—hurry!

Come from the water, Ula, Annan,
Come from the sea, little Morgandy;
Come to the harvest, Devin, Shela,
Leave your songs and poetry.

Ripe corn grows heavy in the field,
Come to the harvest—hurry!
Fruit and nut offer their yield—
Come to the harvest-- hurry

Leave your wolves now, Weylen bold,
Come from your prayers, sweet Maura,
Kegan fire lad, noisy Trystan,
And last comes fair Fionna.

Ripe corn grows heavy in the field,
Come to the harvest—hurry!
Fruit and nut offer their yield—
Come to the harvest-- hurry!

Whispers

In the rustle of the leaves, whispers, whispers;
In the humming of the bees,
Whispers, whispers, whispers.

As the moon drops down in dark, whispers, whispers;
Flying southward croons the lark,
Could that be a whisper?

Late at night the north winds sigh, whispers, whispers;
Gentle voices with them fly,
Do I hear them whisper?

Heed our loved ones from afar, whispers, whispers;
Murmurs floating from the stars,
I can hear them whisper.

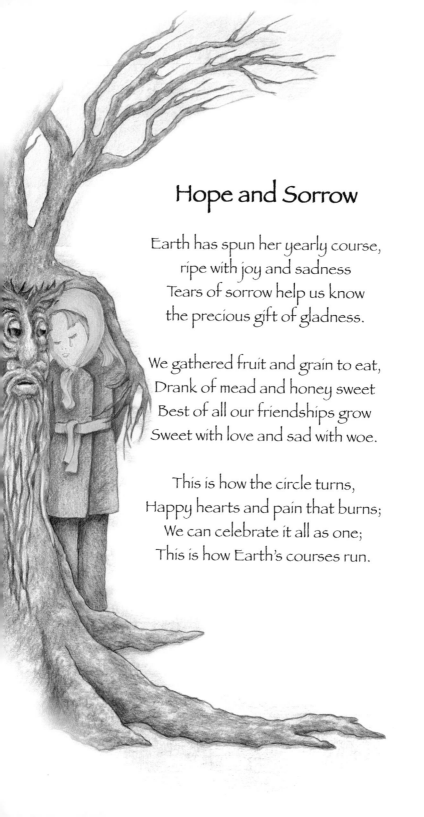

Hope and Sorrow

Earth has spun her yearly course,
ripe with joy and sadness
Tears of sorrow help us know
the precious gift of gladness.

We gathered fruit and grain to eat,
Drank of mead and honey sweet
Best of all our friendships grow
Sweet with love and sad with woe.

This is how the circle turns,
Happy hearts and pain that burns;
We can celebrate it all as one;
This is how Earth's courses run.

Mingled laughter, hope and tears
All together still our fears.
Hope is golden, joy is bright,
Love shines in our saddest night.

Earth has spun her yearly course,
ripe with joy and sadness,
Tears of sorrow help us know
the precious gift of gladness.

Sing in the Darkness, Children

Frost and winter have no hold on the Sun's new birth;
Snow will melt when time is come,
Spring reborn upon our Earth.

Sing in the darkness, Children, sing!
Sing of birds and flowers;
In dark winter we can see
Summer's coming hours.

Frost and winter have no hold on the Sun's new birth;
Snow will melt when time is come,
Spring reborn upon our Earth.

Sing in the darkness, Children, sing!
Sing in storm and gale;
'Though the world in ice is held,
Still, the rising sun we hail!

Frost and winter have no hold on the sun's new birth;
Snow will melt when time is come,
Spring reborn upon our Earth.

The Brave Earth Child's Song

I'm not afraid of anything, anything,
I'm not afraid of anything, anything,
I'm not afraid of anything,
because I'm a child of this Earth.

Fierce fire is my big brother,
Like the wild wind in my hair;
Cool water, my sweet sister,
And the fragrant grass down there.

If I respect the animals,
Then they will respect me;
I honor the sun and the stars and the moon,
And everything that I see.

The lovely sea and big blue sky;
This green and happy land,
There is nothing to fear on earth or sea
In Mother Earth's kind hand.

I'm not afraid of anything, anything,
I'm not afraid of anything, anything,
I'm not afraid of anything,
because I'm a child of this Earth.

Made in the USA
Columbia, SC
05 July 2018